Activities for Sensory Play

Recipes & Ideas for Making Creative Sensory Materials

Kim Beckett

BECKETT PUBLISHING LTD

CONTENTS

INTRODUCTION

 Working as an Early Childhood Educator for over 20 years has taught me that keeping young hands busy and young minds happy is a challenging job. Every successful parent, teacher, or caregiver knows that to have well planned activities for the children in our care is not only exciting for them but also a necessity for a successful activity time. Play dough is one of those indispensable items that a play environment cannot do without.

The Benefits of Sensory Play

As important as blocks, crayons, and paper, play dough will always be a must have in my classroom environments. Materials that support sensory development are a valuable part of a child's play. Sensory play can also support many other important skills like gross and fine motor development, creativity, literacy, social, math and science skills.

Besides the senses we all know, sight, hearing, smell, taste and touch, there are other sensory systems. The proprioception sense is described as the ability to know where our body parts are in relation to each other and the things around us. While playing with dough, children explore this sense, which helps them learn how much force is needed when pulling, pushing or lifting things. The vestibular sense, also known as our sense of balance, is stimulated while

engaged in the intricate manipulations of sculpting and creating. Meaning that during these tabletop activities children are actually learning to keep their balance.

Fine motor development of the hands and fingers is extremely important as preparation for writing, using scissors, painting and other skills that children will be developing.

These are just some of the reasons to include sensory activities in your child's daily activities.

How To Use This Book

The internet has brought so many resources to our fingertips. I honestly don't know how we managed without it. The only downside is it's sometimes hard to find what you're looking for when you need it. This can sometimes be time-consuming.

This book contains some of the best recipes I have found over the years. It has a detailed **Table of Contents** to help you find what you are looking for fast. The recipes are all in one place categorized by their type and numbered, so you can easily find the one you want. There are traditional recipes, some unique play dough recipes, even some edible dough recipes. Also included are some recipes for Slime, Foam and other great materials. Sensory experiences aren't complete without good old sand, so there are even some recipes for that.

In the next section, I will share some great ideas to extend the dough experience. Play dough is always better with special tools and props, like cookie cutters and rolling pins. I will share some popular tools, some you may already have, and others you'll want to get. There is space at the end of this section for you to add tools and props you think of. I encourage you to always be looking for new items to make more of the sensory experience.

Finally, in the last section of the book, there are activities that can help you plan all kinds of sensory play. From dramatic and creative to academic.

I hope this book will become one tool you reach for on the days that you need a bit of inspiration. Let the ideas in this book be your starting place to explore all the fun that these recipes can offer.

Some images in this book have been AI generated, however, most of the pictures I took myself.

The **Resources** section, at the end of the book, contains the links to the fabulous web pages I found through my research. I have personally tested every recipe to make sure it works.

Safety Guidelines

Always be aware of ingredients you're using and the children that will be using them. If you have any children with peanut allergies, you will not be able to use the peanut butter play dough, even if they won't be touching it. There are peanut butter replacements that you can use instead.

Small children might put play dough in their mouth, so using edible play dough might be a better solution in that case.

Play dough, especially hardened pieces, can become choking hazards, so cleaning up after play is very important when little ones are around.

TIPS FOR MAKING SUCCESSFUL DOUGH

Creating the perfect play dough can sometimes be a bit of a science experiment, but with the right tips and tricks, you can achieve that ideal texture every time.

Using old flour can sometimes produce a poor result, so if your dough is not turning out, try using new flour.

Did you know you don't need cream of tartar to make play dough? Its purpose is to preserve the dough and to add an acidic component to stabilize the mixture. It's what makes the play dough soft and pliable. The same amount of lemon juice or vinegar can be substituted to make a successful play dough. The **Kool-Aid Dough** (on page 16) doesn't require cream of tartar because there are acidic ingredients in the Kool-Aid mixture.

Accurate measurements are important. Use measuring cups and spoons to get your recipe just right.

I have found that ingredient amounts can usually be reduced by half if the amounts are too much for your need. To prevent getting the amounts wrong, write the revised amounts down on a sticky note and stick this in the book for the next time.

Combine all dry ingredients first, mixing them well. Gradually add the water while stirring the dough.

When cooking your dough on top of the stove, ensure you are using a low to medium heat to avoid burning the dough. Remove from the heat as soon as it becomes a ball of dough to avoid overcooking it.

If your dough comes out sticky, it might just need more cooking. Heat it up a little longer (5 mins), watching that it doesn't burn.

Sometimes the stickiness goes away after kneading it for a while. Try that first, then either cook a bit more or add a little more flour.

Once the dough is cool enough to handle, we knead it to develop the gluten, the substance that makes the dough stretch.

Let the play dough cool before placing in a sealed container. Sometimes the steam inside the container can turn to water and make the dough wet.

Forming the dough into a ball at the end of play and placing it into an airtight container can help prolong the life of your play dough. If not using the play dough for a while, keep it in the fridge.

When using liquid food coloring, it is easiest to add it to the water before adding the water to the recipe.

If you want more than one color of play dough, don't add the color while making the dough. Once the dough is made, separate it into portions and add the food color to each piece.

To avoid staining your hands when adding color, use plastic gloves or a plastic sandwich bag—just put the dough and dye inside the bag, seal it, and knead until the color is dispersed.

By following these tips, you can create play dough that is soft, pliable, and long-lasting, providing hours of fun for children.

Creating Your Colors

creating the right color for your dough

Red, yellow, and blue, the ***primary colors***, are the foundation of color mixing. Mixing these together will give you the ***secondary colors,*** purple, orange and green. Most of us already know how to get these familiar combinations. Here are a few more color mixtures.

- ORANGE, mix yellow + red

- PURPLE, mix red + blue

- GREEN, mix blue + yellow

- BROWN, mix yellow + red + blue

- DUSTY ROSE, mix 2 drops of blue + 6 drops of red

- MINT GREEN, mix 6 drops of green + 2 drops of yellow

- SUNSET ORANGE, mix 12 drops of yellow + 4 drops of red

- TEAL, mix 6 drops of blue + 4 drops of green

The mixtures above are for using food color for coloring your dough. You can also use gel colors that are used for decorating cakes.

Paints or pigments will produce more vibrant colors. Color can also be created by mixing in all kinds of natural powders for a more earthy color.

Making Your Dough Extra Special

To make traditional dough more exciting, try these additions to the dough after it's made.

Craft Items—glitter, pieces of foil, sequins, plastic gems, plastic pellets, themed items, rice, clean sand, small beads

Essential Oils—Lavender, Rosemary, Peppermint, Pine, Orange, Lemon

Herbs—Lavender, Rosemary, Basil, Lemon Balm, Marjoram, Sage, Thyme, Oregano, Parsley, Chives

Spices—gingerbread spice, pumpkin spice, cloves, mint, curry powder, cinnamon

Flowers—Lavender, Marigolds, Roses, Elderflower, Nasturtiums, Dandelions, Chives, Pansies, Chamomile

Traditional Dough Recipes

Follow the step-by-step instructions for creating a variety of basic play dough recipes. Use measuring cups and spoons to get accurate measurements. Recipes will include tips where necessary to help you have better results.

If your dough doesn't come out right, try the suggestions in the previous chapter **"Tips for Making Successful Dough"**. Sometimes you can easily fix the dough.

As with any skill, making play dough will get easier the more you practice. When you have poor results, let the children play with it, anyway. They will have fun, despite the stickiness or lumpiness.

1. My Favorite Play Dough

This one is my favorite, because it's made in one bowl with boiling water instead of cooking the dough on the burner. Clean up is quick and easy with no messy saucepan to wash. Making play dough in a day care setting where there is no stove is possible with this recipe. I've made this play dough and cleaned up in less than 15 minutes.

Ingredients:

- 1 cup flour

- 1/2 cup salt

- 1 tablespoon cream of tartar

- 1 tablespoon vegetable oil

- 1 cup boiling water

- Food coloring (optional)

Instructions:

In a medium-sized bowl, combine all dry ingredients (flour, salt, and cream of tartar). Mix thoroughly with a fork.

Pour the boiled water into a measuring cup and add the desired food coloring to it.

Stir the colored water into the dry ingredients and mix well.

Add the oil to the mixture and continue to combine the dough until it is all sticking together. When the dough has cooled down enough, you may want to use your hands to press it together, forming one solid ball. Knead it in your hands for a few minutes until it feels smooth.

When the dough has a good consistency, place it in a storage container. While the dough is still warm, it may produce moisture. Keep the lid open to prevent the dough from becoming wet. Close the lid when the dough has cooled.

This play dough can be used for a few weeks, depending on how often it is used. Forming it into a ball each time it's stored will prevent the dough from drying out.

2. Cooked Dough

Ingredients:

- 2 cups flour

- 1 cup salt

- 2 tablespoons cream of tartar

- 2 tablespoons vegetable oil

- 2 cups water

- Food coloring (optional)

Instructions:

In a large saucepan, combine all dry ingredients (flour, salt, and cream of tartar). Mix together thoroughly. If using color, mix it into the water first and then add water and vegetable oil to the dry ingredients.

Cook over medium heat, stirring continuously until the mixture forms a ball and starts to pull away from the sides of the pan. Remove from heat and let it cool slightly.

Knead the dough until smooth. Store in an airtight container.

3. Gluten-Free Dough

Ingredients:

- 1/2 cup rice flour

- 1/2 cup cornstarch

- 1/2 cup salt

- 2 teaspoons cream of tartar

- 1 cup water

- 1 teaspoon vegetable oil

- Food coloring (optional)

Instructions:

In a saucepan, add the rice flour, cornstarch, salt, and cream of tartar. Mix together well.

Add the food coloring to the water (optional). Pour the water and vegetable oil into the dry ingredients. Cook over medium heat, stirring continuously until the mixture thickens and forms a ball.

Remove from heat and let it cool slightly.

Knead until smooth. If desired, food coloring can be added during the kneading process.

Store in an airtight container.

4. Kool-Aid Dough

Ingredients:

- 1 cup flour

- 1/2 cup salt

- 1 tablespoon vegetable oil

- 1 cup water

- 1 packet Kool-Aid mix (for color and scent)

Instructions:

In a saucepan, combine the flour, salt, and Kool-Aid mix.

Add the water and vegetable oil to the dry ingredients.

Cook over low heat, stirring until the mixture forms a ball and starts to pull away from the sides of pan.

Remove from heat, and when it is cool enough, knead the dough until smooth.

Store in an airtight container.

5. Scented Dough

Ingredients:

- 2 cups flour

- 1 cup salt

- 2 tablespoons cream of tartar

- 2 tablespoons vegetable oil

- 2 cups water

- Food coloring (optional)

- Essential oils (lavender, peppermint, etc.)

Instructions:

In a large saucepan, mix together the flour, salt, and cream of tartar.

Add the essential oils to the water. If using food coloring, add it now to the water, as well.

Add the water mixture and vegetable oil to the dry ingredients.

Cook over medium heat, stirring continuously until the mixture is sticking together and pulls away from the sides of the pan.

Remove from the heat and let it cool slightly.

Knead the dough until smooth.

Store in an airtight container.

6. Dough with Natural Powders

In this recipe, the color is created using natural herbs, spices, vegetable, or fruit powders. A few are listed below, but you can use almost any powder you can think of as long as it is safe to ingest. Remember that whatever you are using, it can be absorbed through the skin, so only use powders or spices that will not be harmful or cause sensitivity issues.

Ingredients:

- 1/2 cup flour

- 1/2 cup water

- 2 tablespoons salt

- 1 teaspoon cream of tartar

- Choose from the list below the herb or spice or your choice.

Instructions:

For each batch of play dough, add all the dry ingredients to a saucepan, including the spice or herb you have chosen and mix together.

Add the water and stir.

Cook on medium heat, stirring until the dough forms into a ball. Let cool, knead until smooth.

- Ground Turmeric—1 1/2 teaspoons of turmeric will give your play dough a beautiful yellow color and the smell is amazing.

- Paprika—1 teaspoon of paprika will produce a lovely red color.

- Kale Powder—1 tablespoon will turn your dough into a vibrant green and smell like fresh kale.

- Cocoa Powder—1-2 tablespoons cocoa powder will make a chocolaty dough that smells equally delicious. It might be hard to mix in at first, but keep kneading and it will turn out great.

- Cheddar Cheese Powder—1 tablespoon of this savory powder will make your play dough smell like lunch time. You'll have a cheesy ball of dough when you finish kneading.

- Beet Root—1 teaspoon will create a deep pink color.

- Pitaya—1 tablespoon of this powder from the Dragon Fruit will produce a bright pink dough.

- Matcha—1 tablespoon of this green tea powder will give your dough a deep green color.

- Ground Cinnamon—1 tablespoon of cinnamon will give you a warm spicy light brown colored dough.

Unusual Dough Recipes

The following recipes feature unique textures and ingredients that stimulate sensory experiences.

When you've been making the same old play dough for a while, you may want to try something new. It's easy to create a unique recipe when you follow the basic foundation for dough. You need to have some sort of flour or powder, some type of liquid, and it helps to add some kind of stabilizer. With this in mind, there are limitless ways to vary the ingredients.

Below are some ideas to change the basic ingredients to come up with new recipes of your own. Get creative!

Types of flour/powders include white flour, whole wheat flour, rice flour, corn flour, coconut flour, oat flour (made by grinding oatmeal into a fine powder), and arrowroot powder.

In place of water try, flavored water, carbonated water, orange or lemon juice.

Stabilizers like salt, alum, cream of tartar, lemon, and white vinegar can be used.

Oils—vegetable oils, sunflower oil, coconut oil, baby oil

Colors—food coloring, color gels, paint powder, liquid paint, spices, vegetables

I encourage you and your children to try new things and experiment. Coming up with new recipes is also a creative outlet for children.

7. Sawdust Dough

Ingredients:

- 1 cup sawdust

- 1/2 cup flour

- 1/2 cup boiled water

- 1 tablespoon vegetable oil

- food coloring (optional)

Instructions:

Mix sawdust and flour in a large bowl.

Add food coloring, if desired, to the water.

Gradually add water and vegetable oil while stirring until the mixture forms a dough. You might need more or less water to get the right consistency.

Knead the dough until smooth.

Store in an airtight container.

8. Sand Dough

Ingredients:

- 1 cup of flour

- 1/2 cup of salt

- 1/4 - 3/4 cup of sand

- 2 tablespoons of cream of tartar

- 2 tablespoons of oil

- 1 cup of boiling water

Instructions:

Combine the dry ingredients except the sand, in a mixing bowl and mix well. Add the oil and 1 cup of boiling water.

Stir until dough is forming into a ball. Knead the dough until smooth.

When the dough is a good consistency, add just enough of the sand to coat the outside of the ball of dough and work it in. Do this a few times, each time working the sand into the middle of the dough. The amount of sand will depend on what kind of sand you have. Some sand is more coarse than other types. You will want it to still feel like dough, but have a gritty feel.

Store in an airtight container.

9. Coffee Grounds Dough

Ingredients:

- 1/4 cup coffee grounds

- 1 cup flour

- 1/2 cup salt

- 2 teaspoons cream of tartar

- 1 cup water

- 1 tablespoon vegetable oil

Instructions:

Mix the flour, and salt and cream of tartar in a saucepan.

Over medium heat, stir in the water, oil, and coffee grounds. Mix until the dough begins to form a ball. Remove from heat.

As soon as the dough cools, knead until smooth.

Store in an airtight container.

This makes a heavy, stiffer dough, but it smells wonderful.

10. Mud/Dirt Dough

Ingredients:

- 1 1/2 cups of flour

- 1/2 cup salt

- 1 tablespoon cream of tartar

- 2 tablespoons of vegetable oil

- 1 cup boiling water

- a cup of dirt

Instructions:

Mix the first three ingredients together and slowly add hot water until the dough comes together.

Knead well with your hands, adding a bit more flour if it's too sticky.

When the dough is ready, start mixing in spoonfuls of dirt, one at a time, until you reach the texture you like.

mud/dirt dough

Keeping with the outdoorsy theme, you can add items from nature like stones, twigs and leaves for tools. A planting theme could include some tiny clay pots, tiny spades, and sturdy flower stalks to plant.

This dough should last for a couple of weeks in the fridge.

11. Cloud Dough

Ingredients:

- 1/2 cup hair conditioner

- 1 cup cornstarch

- food coloring (optional)

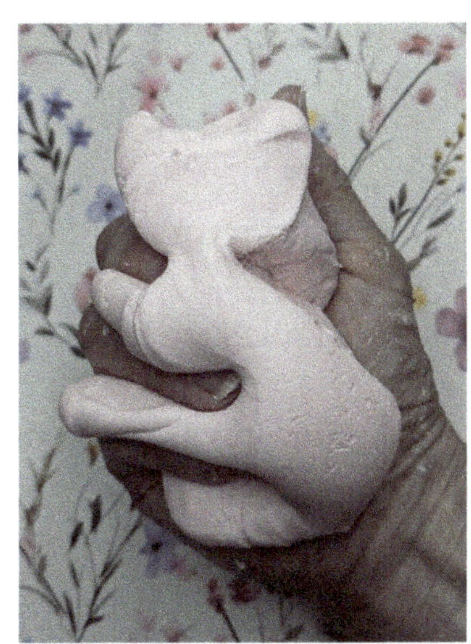

Instructions:

Place the hair conditioner in a bowl. Add the food coloring to the hair conditioner. Stir until well blended. If you want to make more than one color, add the colors after making the dough. Add the cornstarch to the conditioner and mix until it's a good consistency. When it gets difficult to stir, start kneading the dough with your hands.

This dough has a soft texture. Depending on the conditioner you use, it may also have a pleasant scent. To avoid having an overwhelming fragrance, it might be better to use a non-scented variety.

If the consistency is too dry, add a bit more conditioner. If it is too sticky, add a bit more cornstarch.

To clean up, it's better to use a dry cloth instead of a wet one.

This play dough dries out quickly, so it needs to be kept airtight to make it last. It can last up to a week if stored properly. It has a soft, puffy texture.

12. Coconut Dough

Ingredients:

- 1/2 cup flour

- 1/4 cup coconut flour

- 2 tablespoons salt

- 1 teaspoon cream of tartar

- 3/4 - 1 cup water

- shredded coconut (optional)

Instructions:

Place dry ingredients into a saucepan and stir well.

Place over medium heat, pour in 3/4 cup of the water and start stirring. Add more water if needed.

Continue stirring the mixture until the play dough forms a ball.

Place the hot play dough onto wax paper and leave it to cool. When cool, knead it until smooth.

For added texture, add in some shredded coconut.

13. Shaving Foam / Cornstarch Dough

Ingredients:

- 1/2 cup cornstarch

- 1/2 cup shaving foam

- Food coloring (optional)

Instructions:

Place the cornstarch into a bowl.

Add the shaving foam to the cornstarch.

Mix together, adding color if desired.

This is a crumbly dough with a unique texture. It will stick together when pressed firmly, but crumbles quickly.

This dough would make a good pretend sand or snow.

14. Chocolate Dough

Ingredients:

- 2 cups flour

- 2 tablespoons cream of tartar

- 1 cup salt

- 1/2 cup cocoa powder

- 3 tablespoons oil

- 2 cups boiling water

- 4-5 drops vegetable glycerin

Instructions:

Combine the dry ingredients in a bowl, stirring thoroughly. Add the boiling water, one cup at a time.

Mix until fully combined. Add the glycerin and oil, mixing well.

Allow to rest for a few minutes to cool down.

Knead it, to make it softer and more pliable.

Store in an airtight container in the fridge until needed.

15. Oatmeal Dough

Ingredients:

- 1 cup flour

- 1/2 cup salt

- 1 tablespoon cream of tartar

- food coloring (optional)

- 1 cup water (boiled)

- 1 1/2 cups oatmeal

Instructions:

Combine the flour, salt, and cream of tartar.

Add the hot water to the dry ingredients, mixing until the dough is formed.

After kneading the dough, you can start working in the oatmeal by adding a bit at a time until you like the feel.

This play dough doesn't need to be cooked, but by using hot water it will activate the gluten in the dough, making it more pliable.

16. Rubbery Dough

Ingredients:

- 3/4 cup water

- 1/2 cup cornstarch

- 1 cups of baking soda

- 1 tablespoon oil

- food color (optional)

Instructions:

Mix all the dry ingredients together in a saucepan. Add the water while stirring over medium heat.

This dough seems to take longer than flour dough to turn from liquid to solid. When the dough is forming a solid ball and the surface looks dry, remove from heat. Allow to cool.

When cool, add the oil and knead it until smooth. Knead with a spoon until it becomes less sticky. Your patience will be rewarded. This dough has a lovely sparkle, with a different texture than other doughs.

17. Jell-O Dough

Ingredients:

- 1 cup flour

- 1 cup water

- 1/2 cup salt

- 2 tablespoons cream of tartar

- 2 tablespoons vegetable oil

- 1 pkg Jell-O (any flavor)

Instructions:

Mix the flour, salt, cream of tartar, and Jell-O in a saucepan.

Add the water and vegetable oil to the dry ingredients.

Cook over medium heat, stirring continuously until the mixture thickens and forms a ball.

Remove from heat and let it cool. Knead the dough until smooth.

Store in an airtight container in the fridge until needed.

This dough smells good enough to eat, but don't let anyone eat it.

18. Pumpkin Dough

Ingredients:

- 1 cup canned pureed pumpkin

- 1/2 cup water

- 2 tablespoons coconut oil

- 1 teaspoon vanilla

- 1 teaspoon cinnamon

- 1 teaspoon cloves

- 1 teaspoon nutmeg

- 1/2 teaspoon ginger

- Orange food coloring

- 2 1/4 cups flour

- 1/2 cup salt

- 2 tablespoons cream of tartar

Instructions:

In a saucepan, combine the pumpkin, water, oil, food coloring, vanilla, and spices. On medium heat, stir regularly until bubbling. Remove from the heat, allowing to cool slightly.

Combine the dry ingredients in a separate bowl and mix. Add the dry mixture to the pumpkin and stir well. When it is clumping together, place it on a surface to rest for 5-10 minutes.

Start kneading the dough. Knead it until soft and pliable. Be patient, as you work with the dough, it will become less sticky.

Store it in an airtight container in the fridge when not in use. This dough will not last as long as flour and salt dough.

19. Cinnamon Dough

Ingredients:

- 1 cup flour

- 1 tablespoon ground cinnamon

- 1/2 cup salt

- 1/2 cup cold water

- 1 tablespoon vegetable oil

- food coloring

Instructions:

Combine the flour, salt, and ground cinnamon.

Add the cold water and stir until the mixture forms a ball. Place the ball of dough on a surface to rest for a few minutes.

Knead the dough until firm.

Store the dough in an airtight container.

Variations of Cinnamon Dough

You can make variations of this play dough by substituting another spice for the cinnamon.

- gingerbread spices/ brown color

- peppermint/ red or pink color

- rosemary/ cut up rosemary pieces/ dark green color

- pine essential oil/ green color

Taste Friendly Dough Recipes

Safety Concerns

Always be aware of the ingredients you're using when making dough and the children that will be near it. If you have any children with peanut or other food related allergies, you cannot use those ingredients in the play dough, even if the child will not be touching it.

I would recommend that you only use edible play dough when you are using it with your own children, or if you are well acquainted with the children and their health status. If using in a daycare setting, inform parents first and even get written permission.

Although the following few recipes are considered "edible", the dough is for safe sensory exploration, not for food. It is best if you help young children learn the difference between play dough and food.

Most edible play dough recipes have cornstarch as the thickener. Cornstarch is refined from corn and it is not recommended to be eaten raw. If uncooked, it can lead to digestive problems and even blockages.

Explain to the children, even the very young ones, before they play, that the dough is not food. Tell them they can taste it if they want, but it is not to eat. You want them to learn the limits of what can go in their mouth, eventually leading to playing with non-edible play dough.

20. Peanut Butter Dough

Before using this recipe, make sure no children have sensitivities or allergies to Peanut Butter. You can use substitutes instead of using real Peanut Butter.

Ingredients:

- 1 cup smooth peanut butter

- 2 cups powdered sugar

Instructions:

With the peanut butter in a bowl, gradually mix in the powdered sugar until a ball of dough forms.

Knead the ball of dough until it reaches the desired consistency.

To preserve the dough, place it in an airtight container in the fridge. Remember to use it within a few days and then dispose of it, as it is perishable.

Peanut Butter Dough

21. Icing Dough

Ingredients:

- 1 cup ready made cake icing

- 2 cups icing sugar

Instructions:

Mix the icing and the icing sugar in a bowl until it forms a ball of dough. You can add more icing if the dough is too dry.

Knead the dough. Store it in an airtight container in the fridge until needed.

Use only for a few days, as this dough is perishable. If using with more than one child, keep each child's dough separate.

22. Marshmallow Dough

Ingredients:

- 2 oz of marshmallows (see Marshmallow Equivalents Chart in Appendix A)

- 1 tablespoon cornstarch

- 1/2-3/4 cup powdered sugar

- 1 teaspoon coconut oil

Instructions:

Put marshmallows and a bit of water together in a bowl and place in microwave until marshmallows have expanded twice their size (about 20 - 30 seconds).

Add the oil, cornstarch and powdered sugar. Mix it together well.

Knead the dough. Add a little more cornstarch if too sticky. Adding coconut oil to your hands can help at this stage.

Store in an airtight container in the fridge.

During play, putting a bit of coconut oil on the children's hands can help if the play dough is still sticky. If it becomes too hard, you can put it back into the microwave for a few seconds to soften it up again.

This dough is perishable, so using it only once or twice is recommended. When using with more than one child, each child should have their own dough to play with. At the end of play, this dough should be discarded.

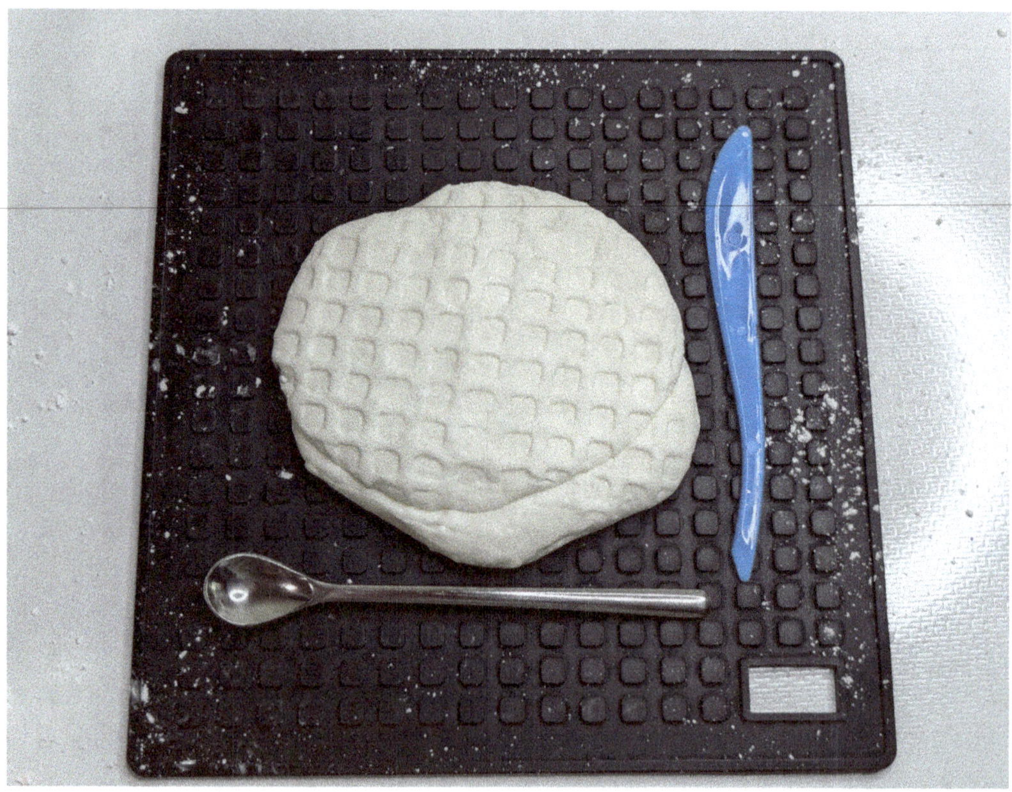

23. Yogurt Dough

Ingredients:

- 1 cup plain yogurt or different flavors if desired

- 3/4 cup cornstarch (more as needed)

Instructions:

Mix the cornstarch and yogurt in a bowl, until it forms a ball of dough. You can add more cornstarch if the dough is too sticky or more yogurt if too dry.

Knead the dough. Store in an airtight container in the fridge, until needed.

Use only for a few days as this dough is perishable. If using with more than one child keep each child's dough separate.

Yogurts vary in their consistency, so you may find, as I did, that you need more cornstarch than is called for in the recipe.

Warning: This recipe contains a high percentage of cornstarch. It is not safe to eat uncooked cornstarch.

Slime Basics

There are many types of sensory mixtures that can provide different stimulating experiences. I've included a few recipes for slime in this book so you can dip your toe in the exciting world of slime. There really is a huge variety when it comes to slime.

Slime is a particularly interesting mixture. The chemistry involved when its ingredients are mixed is fascinating and can also be dangerous. It is important to always use caution and follow the safety guidelines when making these types of mixtures. Used safely, slime can provide children and adults with hours of stimulating fun.

Essential Ingredients of Slime

Slime recipes usually use white school glue or clear glue, which is **Polyvinyl Acetate** or PVA. To make sure it's PVA, put a small amount on paper and let it dry. PVA dries to a clear finish.

Activator—the activator starts a chemical reaction in the glue, causing it to become a new substance. Here are some products you can use as activators.

- Borax mixed in water

- Contact Lens Solution & Baking Soda (make sure the contact lens solution contains boric acid or contains buffered saline)

- Liquid Starch

- Liquid Laundry Detergent (must contain boric acid)

Add-Ins—These are optional. Adding one of the following can change the texture or properties of the slime.

- Glycerin can be added to clear slime to make it more elastic.

- Lotion can be used in place of glycerin to make it more elastic.

- Shaving Foam causes the slime to be more fluffy, but the fluffiness will only last a few days.

- Cornstarch added to white slime helps to thicken it. It also gives it a matte finish.

Slime Safety

Making slime, playing with it, and even handling the ingredients should always be supervised by a responsible adult.

Make sure you know your ingredients and how to handle them safely. If a child or you have a sensitivity to any ingredient, it should not be used. Stop using any ingredient or slime mixture if you notice any skin reactions to it.

Slime mixtures should never be frozen or heated. Always store at room temperature.

Slime or the individual ingredients should never be eaten or placed near eyes, nose or mouth.

Avoid getting slime on sensitive areas like eyes, face, body, or on clothing.

Always place labels on your slime mixtures to avoid them being mistaken for food.

Store slime mixtures and all ingredients out of the reach of children and pets.

Make sure you have good ventilation while making the slime.

Prepare the area where you will make the slime, so that it will not contaminate food preparation or the serving areas. You can use a covered table outside, or completely cover the table you are working on in the kitchen.

Use disposable utensils or separate utensils that are only used for slime making. Never use these for preparing food or use in the bath.

Don't dispose of the mixture down the sink drain. It will solidify and clog up pipes.

Always wash your hands thoroughly with soap and water after making slime or playing with it.

basic clear slime with fine glitter

SLIME & FOAM RECIPES

24. Oobleck (Cornstarch and Water)

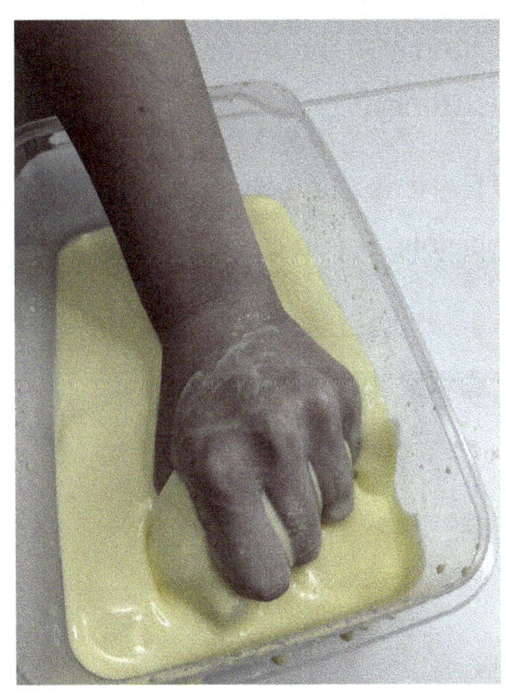

Oobleck has different texture and properties compared to play dough, which makes it more of a slime. Oobleck is technically not a slime, it just fits better here.

The cornstarch mixed with water will form a non-Newtonian fluid (solid when pressed, liquid when relaxed), like quicksand. This interesting combination is sometimes called a suspension. It makes a strange feeling concoction that provides an interesting sensory experience. As the water evaporates out of the mixture, the cornstarch will revert to its solid form.

Did you know? Oobleck got its name from the book Bartholomew and the Oobleck by Dr. Seuss.

Ingredients:

- 1/2 cup water

- 1 cup cornstarch

- Food coloring (optional)

Instructions:

Add food coloring into the cup of water if desired.

Start by adding the water to a large bowl or shallow tray, then mix in the cornstarch slowly until it becomes saturated with the water. You can add more or less water to get the right consistency.

You will know it's perfect when you can feel it as a liquid when you slowly pass your fingers through it and it feels solid if you quickly move your fingers or quickly push down on it.

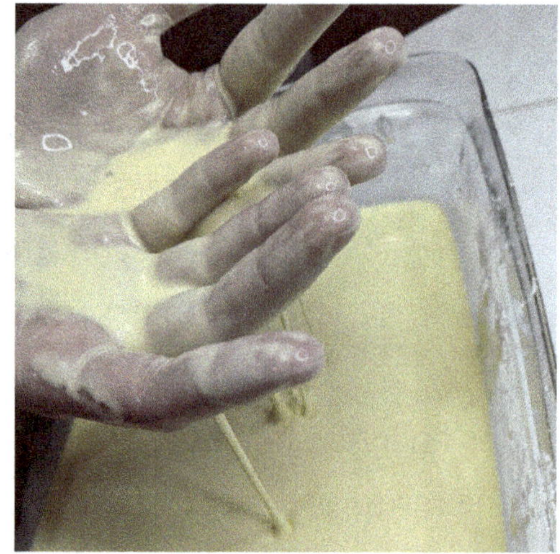

25. Easy Marshmallow Slime

Ingredients:

- 1 1/2 cups of marshmallows

- 1 tablespoon of cornstarch

- 1 tablespoon Vegetable oil

- color is optional

Instructions:

Place the marshmallows in a bowl with a bit of water, and microwave for about 20 seconds, watching it carefully so they don't burn.

When the marshmallows have melted, stir in the cornstarch and mix until it is smooth. It will be very sticky.

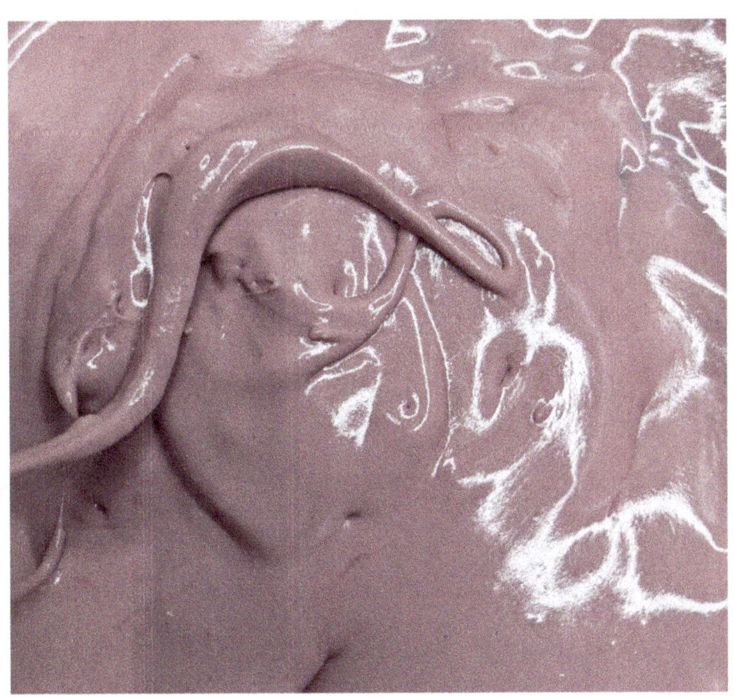

26. Basic Clear Slime

Ingredients:

- 1/2 cup clear glue

- 1/2 cup water

- 1 teaspoon baking powder

- 1 tablespoon + 1/2 teaspoon contact lens solution

- 1 tablespoon fine glitter (optional)

Instructions:

Combine glue and water in a small bowl. Add the baking soda and stir well.

Add the contact lens solution slowly and continually stir as the mixture becomes thick and stringy. Stop adding it as soon as it thickens.

When it comes away from the sides, add the glitter and continue to stir it together until well blended. By now, you should be able to put your fingers in it and pull it up.

If it is still sticky, add a little more contact lens solution.

Keep stretching it with your hands and working with it until it becomes more slime like.

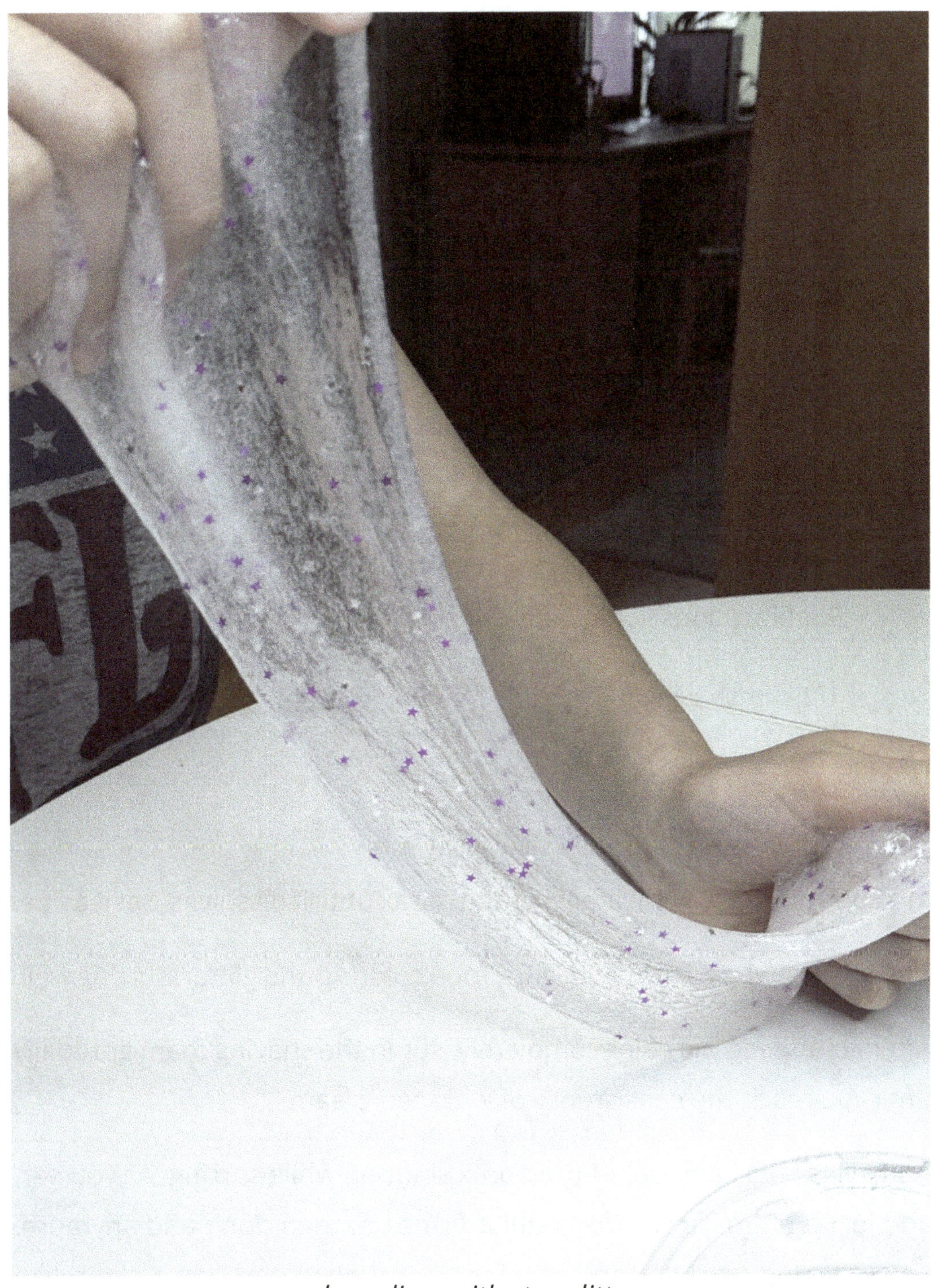

clear slime with star glitter

27. Puffy Slime Recipe

Ingredients:

- 1/3 cup warm water

- 1/2 teaspoon borax

- food coloring and glitter

- 3 tablespoons liquid glue

- 1/2 cup shaving foam

Instructions:

In a cup, mix the warm water with the borax until it dissolves. Set it aside.

In a small bowl, add the white glue, food coloring and glitter, stirring well.

After combining the color completely, stir in the shaving foam gradually until you reach the consistency of whipped cream.

Add just a small amount of the borax solution while stirring. As you stir, add just a bit more solution until it firms up, then don't add anymore. Keep stirring until it stops sticking to the bowl and has a slime like texture.

Work it with your hands until you like the texture. Now you have puffy slime, have fun!

28. Colorful Shaving Foam

Ingredients:

- shaving foam

- food coloring

- muffin pan or ice cube tray

- paintbrushes

- heavy paper or cardstock

Instructions:

Spray the foam into the individual muffin cups in the muffin pan, filling each cup.

Put drops of color into the foam such that each cup contains a different color. See **"Creating Your Colors"** on page 7. Mix each color thoroughly.

Add the paintbrushes and you will have foamy paint to paint pictures with. You can also paint your hand or other objects and make prints on the paper or on a different surface.

29. Shaving Foam Art

Materials:

- white cardstock

- can of shaving foam

- acrylic paint or food coloring

- craft stick or wooden skewer

- squeegee or plastic ruler

- tray

Instructions:

Cut the cardstock into whatever special shape you are creating. You might have hearts for Valentine's day, trees for Christmas, apples or pumpkins for Harvest.

Spray the shaving foam onto the tray. Smooth it all out to have about a 1/2-inch layer of foam covering the tray.

Squeeze the paint or food coloring onto the top of the foam in random patterns. It can be one color or several colors. You can have your children take part in this step.

Show your children how to move the stick or skewer through the foam in different directions to move the paint around in creative ways.

Take your cardstock cutout and lay it on top of the colored foam, making sure it completely contacts the foam. After a few seconds, carefully pick it up from the foam and lay it foam side up on the table.

Take the squeegee or ruler and firmly wipe off the foam. This will leave behind the paint with a beautiful marble effect.

Sand, Snow, Mud & Water

30. DIY Sticky Sand

Ingredients:

5 oz clear glue

1 cup liquid starch

2 lbs. fine sand

Instructions:

Pour the glue and liquid starch into a bowl. Mix this together to make a slime consistency. If it's too thick, add a bit more liquid starch.

Add the liquid, a little at a time, to the sand until you have the right consistency. It should be crumbly but still stick together when pressed.

31. Sensory Sand

Ingredients:

- 1 cup baking soda

- 1/2 cup corn flour

- 1/2 cup decorative sand

- 1 tablespoon cream of tartar

- 1/4 cup water

Instructions:

Combine the dry ingredients in a bowl. Mix well.

Add the water and continue mixing.

This play sand is dry, but sticks together when pressed firmly.

32. Snow Dough

Ingredients:

- 1 cup cornstarch

- 1 cup baking soda

- 2 teaspoons water

Instructions:

Combine the baking soda and cornstarch. Add just a bit of water and mix it in. Keep adding a little water until you are satisfied with the stickiness. It should be a crumbly texture, but be able to be pressed into shapes.

Place the mixture in a tray with a 2-3 inch edge. Children will love this experience with a few tiny snow shovels (spoons), small animals, snowman parts, etc.

33. Snow, the Real Thing

Of course, if you don't have any actual snow available, you'll have to pass on this activity. For those that have snow, here are some great ideas for bringing it indoors and playing with it in different ways.

Ingredients:

- muffin tins, or several small containers

- jug of water

- food color

- several eye droppers

Pour water into all of your containers and add different colors to each one.

Place an eye dropper in each container.

When you have all your materials ready, collect a large bowl of snow from outside.

Place the bowl of snow on a table with the colored water. Let the children squeeze drops of colored water into the snow. It's a short-lived activity as the snow will start melting while they are playing, but they will have fun while it lasts.

Alternatively, you could take the eye droppers and water outside to play where they can do this activity for a longer time.

34. Sand Play

Another wonderful kind of sensory play is good old sand. Every child should have sand to play in. I still remember how much fun I had as a child playing for hours in a sand pit we had in the backyard. We made towns with houses and roads that had cars that went into parking lots and garages. Occasionally, a bucket of water would appear, and then there were lakes and rivers. We never tired of the adventures in the sand.

35. Indoor Mud Puddle

The children will love this. Bring a container of sand or soil into the house and add enough water to make it sludgy. Give your children some tools to scoop and manipulate it and they will play for hours with it. What an easy way to create some indoor fun.

Did you know that soil contains beneficial bacteria?

36. Water Sensory Table Ideas

Children and water, there's just something about water that makes it the ultimate sensory experience. Ideas to make the water experience unique include using themes, having great water toys, and using bubbles or scents.

You'll want to keep your water sensory tools together in a special bin, so they're always available. The water will damage some materials, like pipe cleaners, but don't let that stop you from using them. Just dispose of them if the water ruins them. Most of your tools will be items that can withstand water.

Completely dry your tools before storing them to prevent mold growing.

Basic Water Tools—bubbles, spoons, measuring cups, mechanical hand blender, colander, sponges, turkey basters, funnels, plastic bottles, tongs, sponges, metal strainer, eye droppers, ice cube trays, pool noodles, beads, dish soap

Ideas for Themes

Baking—silicone cupcake holders, pompoms, ice cream scoop, tongs, pretty cake dishes, ribbons, pipe cleaners, spoons, lemon juicer, spatula, large spoons, measuring tools

Washing Dishes—toy dishes, bubbles, cloths, cups, teapot, plastic scrubber

Bathing Babies—plastic dolls, towels, hard soap, luffa, rubber ducky, plastic shampoo bottles

Car Wash—sponges, long-handled brushes, toothbrushes, plastic cars, cloths

Pond—frogs, lily pads, ducks, rocks, fish, seaweed, small turkey basters

Ocean—plastic whales, sharks, boats, pretend coral, plastic gems, shiny stones

Fishing—fishing rods, plastic fish, fishing net, plastic boats

Ice—ice blocks of different colors, artic animals frozen in ice, salt shaker

Science—syringes, beakers, test tubes

Summer—flowers, petals, fancy dishes, spoons, colander, vases, watering can

Essential Tools & Props

Here is a list of different tools and props that can be used with play dough to enhance creativity and playtime organized by where you can buy them or find them. These tools and props can turn a simple play dough session into an engaging and imaginative experience. You'll find space at the end of this chapter to add your own creative tools.

Kitchen Items

- rolling pin—for flattening and smoothing dough

- honey dipper—makes lines in the dough

- cookie cutters—to cut out shapes in various designs

- plastic knives—safe for cutting and slicing dough

- molds—different shapes and sizes for forming dough

- plastic forks and spoons—for creating texture and designs

- toothpicks—for fine details and patterns.

- garlic press—to make spaghetti-like strands

- plastic or wooden spatulas—for lifting and shaping dough

- plastic straws—for cutting out small circles and making holes

- bottle caps—for cutting out circles and creating patterns

- small cookie sheets—to use as a play surface

- silicone cupcake holders—for making cupcakes or holding dough pieces

- silicone molds—for creating different shapes

- birthday candles—for decorating

- small containers—for filling or imprinting

- an empty box of chocolates works great for a Valentine's Day theme.

Office Supplies

- pencils—can be used as a rolling pin, can poke holes through, or as structure for a creation

- paper clips—can be bent in different shapes to function as many tools

- rulers—can cut, make straight lines, measure

- themed erasers—can add to creative fun

- Paper—a background for a play dough masterpiece, and as decorations

Craft Supplies

- stamps—to imprint shapes and patterns

- craft sticks—for shaping and detailing

- glitter, sequins, foil shapes, foam balls,

- popsicle sticks—for sculpting and adding details

- beads—for decorating and embedding in dough

- buttons—to press into dough for designs

- fancy rocks or sea shells—for decorating, or to provide structure

- large bolts—to imprint

- wooden dowels—for rolling and sculpting

Toy Shelves

You can find some of these items in play dough kits sold in toy or craft stores.

- small rolling pins with patterns—to create textured surfaces

- play dough scissors—safe for cutting dough

- textured rolling pins—for adding texture and patterns

- extruder tools—to create long strings or shapes from play dough

- plastic pizza wheel cutter—some have wavy or zigzag edges

- plastic animals and people figures—to create scenes and imprints

- toy hammers—for flattening and imprinting

- lego bricks—to make patterns and imprints

- alphabet and number cutters—for learning and play

- nature items—to decorate or to imprint

- toy cars—to roll over dough and leave tracks

- tiny people from Lego—for dramatic play

- shells and rocks—for natural textures and patterns

- feathers—to create imprints and designs

DIY Play Tools

Don't be afraid to get creative and make your own tools. You can create stamping tools out of just about anything. If you come across interesting patterns or textures on items, collect them in your play dough tools bin. The same applies to molds. Wrap an old woven basket around your rolling pin to turn it into a favorite tool. Before you throw anything away, ask yourself if it could possibly be used as a fun tool.

extruder tool

My List of Play Tools

____

____

____

____

____

Amazing Adventures Playing with Dough

Creative Play Dough Activities

Here's a collection of themed activities that encourage imaginative play, from creating animal figures to building entire play dough cities.

Animal Creations—Place plastic animals in view to inspire children to make their own animal creations. This would make a wonderful introduction into clay modeling.

Play Dough Bakery—Use plastic or real kitchen tools like small pie pans, muffin tins, measuring spoons, fancy plates, bowls, cookie cutters, cookie sheets. Maybe you have a pretend oven to cook them in.

Play Dough Garden—Plastic flowers, fresh greenery, tiny stones, miniature bird bath, small pots and garden tools are some props that can help your child make a beautiful garden.

Play Dough City—To help your child create a cityscape, give them different sizes of square and rectangular molds. Small cars, buses, and police cars can add to the fun.

Nature Impressions—Real leaves, rocks and bark can be used as stamps to make beautiful impressions in the dough.

Hammering Golf Tees—Find a small mallet or hammer and let them hammer the tees into the play dough.

Themed Play Dough Sets

These fun themes can add lots of fun to the play and keep it from getting boring. If you have a theme running in your classroom, this is a great way to include play dough in the theme. Here are some ideas for creating themed sets that can provide imaginative play around specific topics.

Dinosaur Land—Get several plastic dinosaurs, plastic trees, mountains, rocks, ferns and let the children create a prehistoric scene.

Ocean Life Set—Find small fish, octopus, whales, and sharks to help your child play in the ocean. Bits of coral and small pieces of ribbon (seaweed) can make a great ocean.

Other Theme Ideas are Space Exploration, Fairy Tale Characters, Farm Animals Set, Horse Stable, Transportation Set, Insects and Bugs Set, and Holiday Themes.

Learning with Play Dough

Create activities that combine play dough with educational content, helping children learn academic skills through hands-on play.

Shapes—How fun would it be to learn all about shapes with the hands-on experience of play dough? Cookie cutters, and objects as models for shapes, can make this a fun lesson.

Patterns—Understanding patterns is a fundamental math skill. Using play dough for this kind of lesson can help keep it fun and interesting. Show the child how to make their own simple patterns.

Fine Motor Skills Exercises—Showing your young child how to roll play dough into long ropes of dough, or how to roll in a circular pattern to create a ball are some of the basic skills. With a younger child, you will want to play alongside them to model the different ways to manipulate the dough. Children learn by watching others.

Math Skills—With number cookie cutters, have the child make one of each number out of the play dough. Place all numbers horizontally in a row on the table in front of the child. Provide enough small stones (at least 45 for the numbers 1-9) so the child can place the appropriate number of stones under each number. This activity can even incorporate other math skills, such as addition and subtraction.

Alphabet—With a few large, bold letters laminated on sheets of paper, you can have your child fill in the lines of the letter with play dough. Older children that are learning to read can make three-letter words and match them to their appropriate objects.

Color Mixing—With the primary colors of play dough, red, yellow, and blue, show your child how combining the red and blue makes purple, red and yellow makes orange, and blue and yellow makes green. Use the correct language, such as primary colors, and secondary colors, to learn about colors in a fun way.

Sorting Activity—You can easily create a sorting activity by placing different colors of play dough into their matching colored containers or matching different cookie cutter shapes to the same shaped objects or pictures.

Science Experiments—Make a volcano for a "baking soda and vinegar" experiment. Use a cup or bottle and place play dough around the cup to create the volcano. You can even decorate it with paint, sand, and small rocks. Let it air dry for a few days to harden the volcano to make it more authentic. When ready for the experiment, just pour the ingredients into the top of the volcano.

Storytelling—For an interesting way to engage children in story time, you can create story props out of play dough. Later, the children will create and tell their own version of the story.

Play Dough Games

You can play fun and interactive games using dough, promoting social interaction and cooperative play.

Play Dough Pictionary—In this version of the game, you will create the object that is shown on your card as the others try to guess what the object is.

Hide and Seek with Small Toys—One child can hide a toy inside the play dough and another child can try to guess what kind of toy it is.

Play Dough Sculpting Challenge—Everyone makes their best play dough creation. Afterward, the sculptures can be displayed.

Sculpting Challenge - Hamburger

Sensory Play Ideas

Textured Play Dough Creations—adding texture to play dough can be as simple as mixing in some rice, gravel, or sand.

Aromatic Play Dough—adding scent to play dough with essential oils, spices, food, or artificial flavours can enhance the play experience.

Relaxing Music—Play dough makes a great quiet time activity. With some slow classical or instrumental music, it can help everyone wind down at the end of the day. It can make an excellent distraction for an over stimulated little one.

Fidget Tools—You can add play dough or slime mixtures to small balloons to make fidget balls.

Conclusion

Expanding Play is the Goal

In closing, I would like to encourage you to use your creativity and sense of adventure to continue to explore sensory play. Don't be afraid to make mistakes. Some of the most successful creations were at first considered a mistake.

"We don't make mistakes, just happy little accidents."

Bob Ross

Use the ideas in this book as a jumping off point to expand your children's play experiences.

Thank You!

Thank you for reading this book. I hope it will become one of your valuable resources to turn to when you need a new activity.

If you enjoyed this book and found it helpful, I would be very grateful if you would leave your thoughts and feedback of the book on Amazon to help others find it.

You can scan the QR code below or follow the link to go directly to the page where you can do this. You can also get there by going to your account on Amazon and clicking on your purchase.

Link to Amazon.com Book Review Page.

*Amazon.com Book
Review Page*

Link to Amazon.ca Book Review Page

*Amazon.ca Book
Review Page*

RESOURCES

1. "PBS: Public Broadcasting Service."n.d. PBS.Org. https://www.pbs.org/

2. The Foundation Stage Forum Ltd. 2001. "The Foundation Stage Forum Ltd." July 3, 2001. https://eyfs.info/forums

3. Herbs, Mountain Rose. n.d. "Mountain Rose HerbsBlog." https://blog.mountainroseherbs.com/

4. Hwk. 2020. "Home - Housebound With Kids - Craft &Activity Ideas for Kids." Housebound With Kids. November 19, 2020. https://www.houseboundwithkids.com/

5. "The Imagination Tree." n.d. The Imagination Tree. https://theimaginationtree.com/

6. One Little Project. 2024. "One Little Project - Fun Crafts, Easy Recipes, Kids Activities." June 3, 2024. https://onelittleproject.com/

7. The Best Ideas for Kids. 2024. "The Best Ideas for Kids| Art Activities & Craft Projects." July 10, 2024. https://www.thebestideasforkids.com/

8. "Playdough Recipe – the Very Best Homemade PlaydoughRecipe." n.d. https://www.playdoughrecipe.com/

9. Our Best Bites. 2024. "Our Best Bites - Easy,Family-Friendly Recipes for Busy Moms." July 9, 2024. https://ourbestbites.com/

10. "Simply Southern Mom – Travel, Recipes, & Lifestyle With a Southern Touch." Sept 28, 2021. https://www.simplysouthernmom.com/

11. Gibbon,Stacey. 2024. "No Title." Glued to My Crafts. July 1, 2024. https://www.gluedtomycraftsblog.com/

12. Heather,By. 2024. "Fit Mama Real Food – Healthy Family Meal Plans, Easy Real Food Recipes and Healthy Living." Fit Mama Real Food. July 5, 2024. https://www.fitmamarealfood.com/

13. Craftulate.2023. "Craftulate - Find Art, Crafts and Activities for Kids of All Ages. "January 3, 2023. https://craftulate.com/

14. "Home- Mama.Papa.Bubba." 2019. Mama.Papa.Bubba. January 15, 2019. https://mamapapabubba.com/

15. Busy Little Kiddies. 2024b. "Busy Little Kiddies - Fun Activities and Healthy Recipes for Kids." May 30, 2024. https://www.busylittlekiddies.com/

16. Oswald,Stephanie. 2024. "Parenting Chaos." Parenting Chaos. July 9, 2024. https://parentingchaos.com/

17. "Childsplayabc~Nature Is Our Playground." 2024a. Childsplayabc~Nature Is Our Playground.July 10,2024. https://childsplayabc.wordpress.com/

18. Hsu,Agnes. 2024. "Hello, Wonderful - Creative Inspiration, Arts, Crafts &Recipes for Kids - Hello, Wonderful." Hello, Wonderful. July 14, 2024. https://www.hellowonderful.co/

19. "Simply Living Well." 2024. Simply Living Well. May 20,2024. https://simplylivingwell.com/

20. "Messy Little Monster." 2024. Messy Little Monster. July 18, 2024. https://www.messylittlemonster.com/

21. Jane.n.d. "- Kid-friendly Snacks, Lunches and Meals for the Whole Family." https://foodkidslove.com/

22. "Home| a Play Filled Life." n.d. A Play Filled Life. https://www.playfilledlife.com/

23. Staten,Kim. 2024. "FUN Hands-on Preschool and Kindergarten Activities!" Life Over C's.July 12, 2024. https://lifeovercs.com/

24. 2020b. "Home - Housebound With Kids- Craft & Activity Ideas for Kids." Housebound With Kids. November 19,2020. https://www.houseboundwithkids.com/

25. 2021b. "Real Momma | Chasing After the Woman You've Always Been." Real Momma. August 6, 2021. https://realmomma.com/

26. Jackie. 2023. "Home - Pocket of Preschool." Pocket of Preschool. July 31, 2023. https://pocketofpreschool.com/

Front Cover Image by Julietta Watson https://unsplash.com/@jwatson95

APPENDIX 1

MARSHMALLOW EQUIVALENTS CHART

Regular Marshmallows

1 regular marshmallow = .25 ounces = 14 mini marshmallows

8 regular marshmallows = 1 cup

1 cup mini marshmallows = 2 ounces = 8 regular marshmallows

1 jumbo marshmallow = 1 ounce = ½ cup mini marshmallows

1 jumbo marshmallow = 4 regular marshmallows

Mini Marshmallows

1- 10 ounce bag = 6 cups

1- 10 ounce bag = 40 regular marshmallows

1- 16 ounce bag = 8 ½ cups

1- 16 ounce bag of regular marshmallows = 63 marshmallows